Anonymous

Complete List of the Members and Officers of the

Manchester Literary

and Philosophical Society, from its Institution on February 28th, 1781, to

April 28th, 1896

Anonymous

Complete List of the Members and Officers of the Manchester Literary
and Philosophical Society, from its Institution on February 28th, 1781, to April 28th,
1896

ISBN/EAN: 9783337075927

Printed in Europe, USA, Canada, Australia, Japan

Cover: Foto ©ninafisch / pixelio.de

More available books at **www.hansebooks.com**

Complete List of the Members & Officers

OF THE

MANCHESTER

LITERARY AND PHILOSOPHICAL

SOCIETY,

FROM ITS INSTITUTION ON FEBRUARY 28th, 1781,
TO APRIL 28th, 1896.

AND

Bibliographical Lists of the Manuscript Volumes dealing
with the affairs of the Society,

AND OF THE

Volumes of the Memoirs and Proceedings
Published by the Society.

WITH TWO APPENDICES.

MANCHESTER:
36, GEORGE STREET.
—
1896.

PREFACE.

WHEN the Council of the Society resolved, some time ago, that a complete list, up to the date of issue, of the members of the Society and of its Officers should be prepared for publication, it was thought that it would not involve more labour than that of adding to the list in Dr. Angus Smith's Centenary Volume the names which have accrued since 1881. As soon, however, as the work was begun, it was found necessary to examine the records of the Society carefully anew. Lapse of time has made it difficult to identify some of the earlier members, and it is to be regretted that the publication of a list was not attempted at an earlier date in the Society's history. Any information regarding the members which this publication may elicit will be welcomed. The intention has been to find out the full names of all the members and to identify them as far as possible. With this view, distinctive degrees and titles have been given, when they are known, and the descriptive term *senior* or *junior* has been retained when it seems to serve this purpose.

It is hoped that the examination of the records has disclosed some matters of interest to members, notably in the determination, with only one case of uncertainty, of

Nov. 5th, 1896.

the names of the founders of the Society in 1781. In the
preface of the first volume of Memoirs (1785) it is stated
that the Society, as instituted in 1781, originated in the
meeting of a few gentlemen, inhabitants of the town, as
a kind of weekly club for the purpose of conversing on
subjects of literature and philosophy, which continued for
some years, and which grew in membership so far as to
induce the Founders of the Society to think of extending
their original design. No authentic list of these gentlemen is known to exist, and it is necessary to indicate the
nature of the evidence in our possession on which the list
here given is constructed.

In general, the evidence of membership is the record
of election in the MS. Journal of the Society in its earlier
days, and in the Proceedings of the Society since these
have been published. In addition, we have the book
for the proposal of candidates, from which we have dis-
covered the full names of many who have proposed others
as members, and, finally, the Treasurer's Account Books.
At the commencement, there is no separate Candidates'
Book, nor any Treasurer's Book, as no such officer was
elected till 1783, and we have to depend solely on the
MS. Journal.

The first volume of this Journal begins with the initiatory
meeting on February 28th, 1781, but, beyond the date, it
records only the election of Presidents and Secretaries. This
is followed by a list of members, which consists of an
original list of names, under the several initial letters on
separate pages, with the names added of all those elected
during the period, from February 28th, 1781, to February
13th, 1782, over which the record in the volume extends.
Four of these names are, however, struck out. Proceeding
with the description of the volume, there is no record of
any meeting being held on March 7th, but a record of
attendance and of the proceedings is given for the 14th,
21st, and 28th of March. For the next three meetings no

record of attendance is kept. On the whole, the minutes appear to be sufficiently recorded. The page containing the proceedings of the meeting on June 6th, 1781, has been torn out. In the minutes, the resignations of three out of the four whose names are struck out of the list of members are recorded, but not of the fourth; of course, it might have been minuted on the missing page.

However, the Secretaries of the time have reversed the book, and made use of the last pages for keeping some accounts. Counting from this end, the first page records the receipt of subscriptions over a period from the commencement to (about) July, 1781. The second page contains some items of expenditure, obviously incomplete. The third page contains a list of subscriptions beginning in October, 1781.

The value of these subscription lists as evidence turns upon their completeness. On examination the only name missing is that of the gentleman, Mr. Uniach, whose name is struck out of the list of members, and whose resignation is not recorded. With this one exception, the Journal supplies us with the list of Founders, but the exception is important since Mr. Uniach was present at the first three meetings, and, though his name does not occur again, appears to be connected in some way with the group of men who founded the Society.

The connection may be one of relationship. A John Uniacke,* of Youghal, co. Cork, married the eldest daughter of Roger Manwaring, and succeeded to some portion of the family estates of the Manwarings at Kermincham (and Dr. Mainwaring was in the remainder). His son, John Manwairing Uniacke, born in 1762, entered the Manchester Grammar School in 1774, and would be 19 years of age at the time in question. To explain the record, it is suggested that John Uniacke (Uniach) may have been introduced

* Manchester School Register, Vol. I., p. 199.

as a visitor by his relative Dr. Peter Mainwaring, and
that his name may have been inserted among the members
in error.

Treating this as the correct explanation, a very interesting group of men is found who can be regarded, without
hesitation, as the originators of the Society. Their names
are given at the end of this preface.

The names in the subjoined list are placed in alphabetical
order, as it thus best serves the purpose of an index. For
other purposes, the arrangement by priority of election might
be better, the founders would then head the list, and the new
members in successive years would follow. This method
would shew, among other things, the rise and fall in the
recruiting of the Society, and, to some extent, the changes in
the recruiting ground. Even as it stands, the preparation
of the list has made manifest to how great an extent the
personal constitution of the Society has been modified, and
even transformed, by the growth of the town and the tendency
to live at greater distances from its centre. And it seems
hardly less than certain that, in process of time, the effect
would have been to cause the extinction of the Society had it
not been, to some extent, counterbalanced by the growth of
educational establishments and the increasing demand for
scientific experts in the different industries of the district.
The consequence has been that while the number of members
professionally engaged in scientific pursuits, either as investi-
gators or teachers, has increased, there is a considerably
smaller number of members engaged in business who either
possess a taste for scientific knowledge themselves or are
desirous of encouraging others in its pursuit. Considering
the debt which Manchester owes to scientific progress gene-
rally, and to the scientific work of members of this Society in
particular, this cannot fail to be a matter of regret. More-
over, a portion of the plain intention of the founders is thus
being defeated, and the Society has suffered partly by the
reduction of its immediate sphere of influence, and partly

by the loss of membership, and, consequently, of income, on which its ability to continue the publication of Memoirs, and to maintain the utility of the Library depends. A glance through the list will show how much of what has been best in Manchester has at all times been attracted into the membership of this Society, and, if interest is aroused by reading it, details of the life and work of several members will be found in Dr. Angus Smith's Centenary Volume.

A bibliographical list of the MS. volumes dealing with the affairs of the Society, which have been used in the preparation of the lists, and of the several publications of the Society, is printed after the lists. And, as appendices, are reprinted the two earliest publications of the Society, of which, beyond the copies in the British Museum, a single example of the first only is known at present to be in existence.

NAMES OF THE ORIGINAL MEMBERS

WHO FOUNDED THE SOCIETY,

FEBRUARY 28TH, 1781.

Rev. Thomas Barnes, D.D.
Thomas Butterworth Bayley, F.R.S.
George Bell, M.D.
George Bew, M.D.
John Drinkwater, M.D.
Alexander Eason, M.D.
Robinson Foxley, M.D.
Richard Edward Hall.
Edward Hall.
Richard Hall.
Thomas Henry, F.R.S.
Peter Mainwaring, M.D.
James Massey.
John Massey.
Joshua Oldham.
Thomas Percival, M.D., F.R.S., F.S.A
Charles de Polier (Bottens).
William Reid.
Captain William Roberton.
—— Thomas.
George Wakefield.
Charles White, F.R.S.
William White.
John Wright, M.D.

LIST OF OFFICERS AND MEMBERS.

PRESIDENTS.

Date of Election.

1781. Peter Mainwaring, M.D., James Massey.
1782-1786. James Massey, Thomas Percival, M.D., F.R.S.
1787-1789. James Massey.
1789-1804. Thomas Percival, M.D., F.R.S.
1805, 1806. Rev. George Walker, F.R.S.
1807-1809. Thomas Henry, F.R.S.
1809. *John Hull, M.D., F.L.S.
1809-1816. Thomas Henry, F.R.S.
1816-1844. John Dalton, D.C.L., F.R.S.
1844-1847. Edward Holme, M.D., F.L.S.
1848-1850. Eaton Hodgkinson, F.R.S., F.G.S.
1851-1854. John Moore, F.L.S.
1855-1859. Sir William Fairbairn, Bart., LL.D., F.R.S.
1860, 1861. James Prescott Joule, D.C.L., F.R.S.
1862, 1863. Edward William Binney, F.R.S., F.G.S.
1864, 1865. Robert Angus Smith, Ph.D., F.R.S.
1866, 1867. Edward Schunck, Ph.D., F.R.S.
1868, 1869. James Prescott Joule, D.C.L., F.R.S.
1870, 1871. Edward William Binney, F.R.S., F.G.S.
1872, 1873. James Prescott Joule, D.C.L., F.R.S.
1874, 1875. Edward Schunck, Ph.D., F.R.S.
1876, 1877. Edward William Binney, F.R.S., F.G.S.
1878, 1879. James Prescott Joule, D.C.L., F.R.S.
1880, 1881. Edward William Binney, F.R.S., F.G.S.
1882, 1883. Sir Henry Enfield Roscoe, D.C.L., F.R.S.
1884, 1885. William Crawford Williamson, LL.D., F.R.S.
1886. Robert Dukinfield Darbishire, B.A., F.G.S.
1887. Balfour Stewart, LL.D., F.R.S.
1888, 1889. Osborne Reynolds, LL.D., F.R.S.
1890, 1891. Edward Schunck, Ph.D., F.R.S.
1892, 1893. Arthur Schuster, Ph.D., F.R.S.
1894, 1895. Henry Wilde, F.R.S.
1896. Edward Schunck, Ph.D., F.R.S.

* Elected April 23; resigned office May 5.

VICE-PRESIDENTS.

1781.   Thomas Percival, M.D., F.R.S., Rev. Thomas Barnes, D.D., Thomas Butterworth Bayley, F.R.S., and Alexander Eason, M.D.

1782.   Rev. Samuel Hall, M.A., John Cowling, M.D., Rev. Thomas Barnes, D.D., and Alexander Eason, M.D.

1783, 1784.   Rev. Thomas Barnes, D.D., Alexander Eason, M.D., Rev. Samuel Hall, M.A., and Charles White, F.R.S.

1785.   Rev. Samuel Hall, M.A., Charles White, F.R.S., George Lloyd, and George Bew, M.D.

1786, 1787.   Rev. Samuel Hall, M.A., Thomas Cooper, Charles White, F.R.S., and George Lloyd.

1788, 1789.   Rev. Samuel Hall, M.A., Charles White, F.R.S., Thomas Cooper, and Thomas Henry, F.R.S.

1790, 1791.   Thomas Cooper, Thomas Henry, F.R.S., Charles White, F.R.S., and Sir George Philips, Bart.

1792.   Charles White, F.R.S., Thomas Henry, F.R.S., John Ferriar, M.D., and Sir George Philips, Bart.

1793-1796.   Charles White, F.R.S., Thomas Henry, F.R.S., John Ferriar, M.D., and Rev. John Radcliffe, M.A.

1797.   Charles White, F.R.S., Samuel Argent Bardsley, M.D., Thomas Henry, F.R.S., and John Ferriar, M.D.

1798-1806.   Charles White, F.R.S., Samuel Argent Bardsley, M.D., Thomas Henry, F.R.S., and Edward Holme, M.D., F.L.S.

1807, 1808.   Edward Holme, M.D., F.L.S., Samuel Argent Bardsley, M.D., Peter Mark Roget, M.D., F.R.S., and William Henry, M.D., F.R.S.

1809-1811.   Edward Holme, M.D., F.L.S., Benjamin Gibson, John Dalton, D.C.L., F.R.S., and William Henry, M.D., F.R.S.

1812-1816.   Edward Holme, M.D., F.L.S., William Henry, M.D., F.R.S., John Dalton, D.C.L., F.R.S., and Peter Ewart.

1817-1821.   Edward Holme, M.D., F.L.S., William Henry, M.D., F.R.S., Peter Ewart, and Rev. William Johns.

1822-1835.   Edward Holme, M.D., F.L.S., William Henry, M.D., F.R.S., Peter Ewart, and George William Wood, F.L.S., F.G.S.

1836.   Edward Holme, M.D., F.L.S., William Henry, M.D., F.R.S., George William Wood, F.L.S., F.G.S., and Charles Phillips, M.D.

1837.   Edward Holme, M.D., F.L.S., George William Wood, F.L.S., F.G.S., Charles Phillips, M.D., and William Charles Henry, M.D., F.R.S.

Date of Election.

1838-1842. Edward Holme, M.D., F.L.S., George William Wood, F.L.S., F.G.S., Rev. John James Tayler, B.A., and John Moore, F.L.S.

1843. Edward Holme, M.D., F.L.S., George William Wood, F.L.S., F.G.S., John Moore, F.L.S., and Peter Clare, F.R.A.S.

1844. Edward Holme, M.D., F.L.S., John Moore, F.L.S., Peter Clare, F.R.A.S., and Joseph Atkinson Ransome, F.R.C.S.

1845-1847. John Moore, F.L.S., Peter Clare, F.R.A.S., Joseph Atkinson Ransome, F.R.C.S., and Eaton Hodgkinson, F.R.S., F.G.S.

1848. John Moore, F.L.S., Peter Clare, F.R.A.S., Joseph Atkinson Ransome, F.R.C.S., and John Davies, M.W.S.

1849, 1850. John Moore, F.L.S., Peter Clare, F.R.A.S., Joseph Atkinson Ransome, F.R.C.S., and Sir William Fairbairn, Bart., LL.D., F.R.S.

1851. Sir William Fairbairn, Bart., LL.D., F.R.S., James Prescott Joule, D.C.L., F.R.S., Laurence Buchan, and Joseph Chesborough Dyer.

1852-1854. Sir William Fairbairn, Bart., LL.D., F.R.S., Joseph Chesborough Dyer, Eaton Hodgkinson, F.R.S., F.G.S., and James Prescott Joule, D.C.L., F.R.S.

1855. James Prescott Joule, D.C.L., F.R.S., Joseph Chesborough Dyer, Eaton Hodgkinson, F.R.S., F.G.S., and Thomas Hopkins.

1856. James Prescott Joule, D.C.L., F.R.S., Joseph Chesborough Dyer, Thomas Hopkins, and Edward William Binney, F.R.S.

1857. James Prescott Joule, D.C.L., F.R.S., Joseph Chesborough Dyer, Thomas Hopkins, and Alexander John Scott, M.A.

1858. James Prescott Joule, D.C.L., F.R.S., Joseph Chesborough Dyer, Thomas Hopkins, and James Crossley, F.S.A.

1859. James Prescott Joule, D.C.L., F.R.S., Thomas Hopkins, Joseph Chesborough Dyer, and Robert Angus Smith, Ph.D., F.R.S.

1860, 1861. Sir William Fairbairn, Bart., LL.D., F.R.S., Robert Angus Smith, Ph.D., F R.S., Joseph Chesborough Dyer, and Edward William Binney, F.R.S.

1862, 1863. James Prescott Joule, D.C.L., F.R.S., Robert Angus Smith, Ph.D., F.R.S., Joseph Chesborough Dyer, and Edward Schunck, Ph.D., F.R.S.

1864, 1865. James Prescott Joule, D.C.L., F.R.S., Edward William Binney, F.R.S., Joseph Chesborough Dyer, and Edward Schunck, Ph.D., F.R.S.

1889. William Crawford Williamson, LL.D., F.R.S., Edward Schunck, Ph.D., F.R.S., James Prescott Joule, D.C.L., F.R.S., and Arthur Schuster, Ph.D., F.R.S.

1890, 1891. William Crawford Williamson, LL.D., F.R.S., Osborne Reynolds, LL.D., F.R.S., Arthur Schuster, Ph.D., F.R.S., and James Bottomley, B.A., D.Sc.

1892, 1893. Edward Schunck, Ph.D., F.R.S., Osborne Reynolds, LL.D., F.R.S., James Bottomley, B.A., D.Sc., and James Cosmo Melvill, M.A., F.L.S.

1894. Edward Schunck, Ph.D., F.R.S., Osborne Reynolds, LL.D., F.R.S., Arthur Schuster, Ph.D., F.R.S., and James Cosmo Melvill, M.A., F.L.S.

1895. Edward Schunck, Ph.D., F.R.S., Osborne Reynolds, LL.D., F.R.S., Arthur Schuster, Ph.D., F.R.S., and Francis Nicholson, F.Z.S.

1896. Osborne Reynolds, LL.D., F.R.S., Arthur Schuster, Ph.D., F.R.S., James Cosmo Melvill, M.A., F.L.S., and Charles Bailey, F.L.S.

SECRETARIES.

1781-1784. Thomas Henry, F.R.S., and George Bew, M.D.

1785, 1786. Rev. Thomas Barnes, D.D., and Thomas Henry, F.R.S.

1787. Thomas Henry, F.R.S., and John Ferriar, M.D.

1788. John Wynne and John Ferriar, M.D.

1789, 1790. John Ferriar, M.D., and James Watt, jun.

1791. John Ferriar, M.D., and William Simmons.

1792. William Simmons and Thomas Henry, jun.

1793. Samuel Harvey and Samuel Argent Bardsley, M.D.

1794-1796. Samuel Argent Bardsley, M.D., and Edward Holme, M.D., F.L.S.

1797. Edward Holme, M.D., F.L.S., and William Henry, M.D., F.R.S.

1798, 1799. John Hull, M.D., F.L.S., and William Henry, M.D., F.R.S.

1800-1806. John Hull, M.D., F.L.S , and John Dalton, D.C.L., F.R.S.

1807, 1808. John Dalton, D.C.L., F.R.S., and Rev. William Johns.

1809. Rev. William Johns and William Winstanley, M.D.

1810-1816. Rev. William Johns and John Atkinson Ransome, F.R.C.S.

1817-1820. John Atkinson Ransome, F.R.C.S., and Thomas Henry Robinson.

Date of Election.

1821.   Thomas Henry Robinson and Peter Clare, F.R.A.S.

1822-1837.   Peter Clare, F.R.A.S., and Rev. John James Tayler, B.A.

1838-1842.   Peter Clare, F.R.A.S., and Joseph Atkinson Ransome, F.R.C.S.

1843.   Joseph Atkinson Ransome, F.R.C.S., and John Davies, M.W.S.

1844, 1845.   John Davies, M.W.S., and John Holt Stanway, F.R.A.S.

1846, 1847.   John Davies, M.W.S., and James Prescott Joule, D.C.L., F.R.S.

1848-1850.   James Prescott Joule, D.C.L., F.R.S., and Edward William Binney, F.R.S., F.G.S.

1851.   Edward William Binney, F.R.S., F.G.S., and Rev. Henry Halford Jones, F.R.A.S.

1852-1854.   Rev. Henry Halford Jones, F.R.A.S., and Robert Angus Smith, Ph.D., F.R.S.

1855, 1856.   Robert Angus Smith, Ph.D., F.R.S., and Edward Schunck, Ph.D., F.R.S.

1857-1859.   Edward Schunck, Ph.D., F.R.S., and Richard Copley Christie, M.A.

1860.   Edward Schunck, Ph,D., F.R.S., and Sir Henry Enfield Roscoe, D.C.L., F.R.S.

1861-1873.   Sir Henry Enfield Roscoe, D.C.L., F.R.S., and Joseph Baxendell, F.R.S., F.R.A.S.

1874-1883.   Joseph Baxendell, F.R.S., F.R.A.S., and Osborne Reynolds, LL.D., F.R.S.

1884.   Joseph Baxendell, F.R.S., F.R.A.S., and James Bottomley, B.A., D.Sc.

1885.   James Bottomley, B.A., D.Sc., and Arthur Schuster, Ph.D., F.R.S.

1886, 1887.   Arthur Schuster, Ph.D., F.R.S., and Frederick James Faraday, F.L.S.

1888-1895.   Frederick James Faraday, F.L.S., and Reginald Felix Gwyther, M.A.

1896.   Reginald Felix Gwyther, M.A., and Francis Jones, F.C.S., F.R.S.E.

TREASURERS.

LIBRARIANS.

ORDINARY MEMBERS.

(F. denotes one of the Founders of the Society.)

Date of Election.

Jan. 27, 1857.	Acton, Henry Morell, B.A.
Nov. 13, 1888.	Adams, Charles Norrish, B.A.
Jan. 11, 1881.	Adamson, Daniel, M.Inst.C.E., F.G.S.
April 29, 1856.	Adshead, Joseph.
Jan. 25, 1805.	Ainsworth, James.
April 30, 1839.	Ainsworth, Ralph Fawsett, M.D., M.R.C.S.
May 2, 1800.	Ainsworth, Thomas.
Jan. 26, 1847.	Albert, Dominic Fric, LL.D.
Jan. 22, 1861.	Alcock, Thomas, M.D., M.R.C.S.
Nov. 15, 1870.	Aldis, Thomas Steadman, M.A.
Jan. 24, 1854.	Allan, James, Ph.D., M.A.
Nov. 4, 1884.	Allen, Bulkeley.
Jan. 7, 1873.	Allmann, Julius.
April 19, 1821.	Andrew, Robert.
Dec. 13, 1870.	Angell, John, F.C.S.
Jan. 22, 1861.	Anson, Rev. George Henry Greville, M.A.
Jan. 21, 1896.	Armstrong, Frank.
Jan. 8, 1895.	Armstrong, George Booth.
Nov. 17, 1885.	Armstrong, Thomas, F.R.M.S.
Jan. 24, 1882.	Arnold, William Thomas, M.A.
April 17, 1849.	Ash, William Henry.
Oct. 29, 1824.	Ashton, Thomas, M.D.
Aug. 11, 1837.	Ashton, Thomas, LL.D.
Oct. 18, 1881.	Ashton, Thomas Gair, M.A.
Feb. 18, 1862.	Ashworth, Henry.
Dec. 26, 1781.	Ashworth, James.
Oct. 31, 1871.	Ashworth, John.
Nov. 16, 1887.	Ashworth, John Jackson.
Nov. 4, 1796.	Ashworth, Robert.
Nov. 2, 1792.	Atkinson, John.
Jan. 27, 1846.	Atkinson, John, F.G.S.
Jan. 14, 1784.	Atkinson, Joseph.
Jan. 22, 1813.	Atkinson, Thomas.
Jan. 27, 1804.	Atkinson, William.
Nov. 3, 1874.	Axon, William Edward Armytage, F.R.S.L., F.S.S.
Nov. 14, 1865.	Bailey, Charles, F.L.S.
Nov. 13, 1888.	Bailey, George Herbert, D.Sc., Ph.D., F.C.S.
Feb. 7, 1888.	Bailey, Sir William Henry, M.Inst.M.E.
Oct. 16, 1883.	Baker, Harry, F.C.S.

Date of Election.

Nov. 15, 1786.	Baker, Joseph.
April 26, 1822.	Baker, Richard George.
Oct. 19, 1821.	Bamber, Richard Parr.
April 30, 1824.	Bannerman, Henry.
Jan. 23, 1824.	Barbour, Robert.
Dec. 10, 1790.	Bardsley, Samuel Argent, M.D.
Oct. 31, 1794.*	Barker, ——
Nov. 14, 1865.	Barker, Thomas, M.A.
Jan. 27, 1852.	Barlow, Henry Bernoulli.
Oct. 29, 1844.	Barlow, William.
Jan. 8, 1895.	Barnes, Charles Lightfoot, M.A., F.C.S.
F.	Barnes, Rev. Thomas, D.D.
Jan. 24, 1834.	Barratt, James, jun.
April 19, 1842.	Barratt, Joseph.
Nov. 28, 1876.	Barratt, Walter Edward.
Nov. 10, 1797.	Barrett, Charles.
Feb. 15, 1786.	Barritt, Thomas.
May 23, 1781.	Barrow, John.
Nov. 12, 1867.	Barrow, John, F.S.A.
Jan. 22, 1819.	Barrow, Peter.
Jan. 24, 1806.	Barton, Horatio.
Jan. 24, 1834.	Barton, Samuel.
April 17, 1849.	Bassnett, Rev. Richard, M.A.
Jan. 21, 1840.	Bateman, John Frederic, F.R.S., M.Inst.C.E.
Jan. 26, 1858.	Baxendell, Joseph, F.R.S., F.R.A.S.
F.	Bayley, Thomas Butterworth, F.R.S.
Jan. 23, 1801.	Bayley, William Kennedy.
Oct. 30, 1812.	Bayliff, William.
Jan. 26, 1847.	Bazley, Sir Thomas, Bart. (M.P.)
April 19, 1853.	Bazley, Sir Thomas Sebastian, Bart., M.A.
Jan. 8, 1889.	Beard, James Rait.
Jan. 26, 1827.	Beard, Rev. John Relly, D.D.
April 16, 1867.	Beasley, Henry Charles.
Feb. 11, 1803.	Becher, Charles Christian.
Nov. 27, 1877.	Becker, Wilfred, B.A.
Jan. 9, 1894.	Beckett, John Hampden, B.Sc., F.C.S.
Nov. 26, 1878.	Bedson, Peter Phillips, D.Sc., F.C.S.
April 30, 1839.	Beeston, William Calvert.
Jan. 25, 1833.	Beever, James Frederick.
April 14, 1896.	Behrens, George Benjamin.
Mar. 5, 1895.	Behrens, Gustav.
Jan. 25, 1848.	Bell, Charles, M.D.

* This date, as given in the Candidates' Book, is evidently erroneous.

Date of Election.

F.	Bell, George, M.D.
Nov. 15, 1870.	Bell, Joseph Carter, F.C.S.
Jan. 26, 1847.	Bell, William.
April 21, 1857.	Bellhouse, Edward Taylor.
April 11, 1781.	Bennet, Rev. John.
Nov. 15, 1870.	Bennion, John Alexander, M.Sc., F.R.A S.
Jan. 26, 1858.	Benson, Davis.
April 26, 1799.	Bentley, Gartside.
April 16, 1829.	Bentley, John.
Mar. 22, 1786.	Bentley, Michael.
April 30, 1830.	Bently, Rev. Thomas Rothwell, M.A.
Jan. 23, 1844.	Bevan, James.
F.	Bew, George, M.D.
Jan. 24, 1854.	Beyer, Charles Frederick.
Dec. 15, 1868.	Bickham, Spencer Henry, F.L.S.
Feb. 12, 1783.	Bill, John.
April 14, 1896.	Bindloss, James Backhouse.
Jan. 25, 1842.	Binney, Edward William, F.R.S., F.G.S.
Jan. 26, 1838.	Binyon, Alfred.
Jan. 16, 1782.	Birch, John.
Nov. 15, 1870.	Bird, John Durham, M.D.
April 27, 1804.	Birley, Hugh Hornby.
Jan. 24, 1823.	Birley, Richard.
April 18, 1834.	Birley, Richard.
April 18, 1876.	Birley, Thomas Hornby.
April 30, 1839.	Black, James, M.D., F.G.S.
Jan. 26, 1821.	Blackwall, John, F.L.S.
Jan. 25, 1842.	Blake, George, M.A.
April 28, 1896.	Bolton, Herbert, F.R.S.E.
Jan. 27, 1837.	Boothman, Thomas, sen.
Oct. 29, 1824.	Boothman, Thomas, jun.
Jan. 22, 1861.	Bottomley, James, B.A., D.Sc., F.C.S.
April 29, 1796.	Boutflower, John Johnson.
April 23, 1855.	Bowman, Eddowes, M.A.
Jan. 22, 1889. } Feb. 18, 1896. }	Bowman, George, M.D.
Oct. 29, 1839.	Bowman, Henry.
Jan. 25, 1842.	Bowman, John.
April 17, 1838.	Bowman, John Eddowes, F.L.S., F.G.S.
Nov. 16, 1875.	Boyd, John.
April 18, 1834.	Brackenbury, James Blackledge.
Oct. 15, 1889.	Bradley, Nathaniel, F.C.S.
Oct. 22, 1783.	Brandt, Charles Frederick.

* No record of election, but appears in list of members published in Vol. IV. pt. 1 of the " Memoirs " (1793).

Date of Election.

April 25, 1806.	Corrie, Edward.
Jan. 25, 1853.	Cottam, Samuel, F.R.A.S.
Oct. 20, 1837.	Cottam, Samuel Elsworth, F.R.A.S.
Jan. 25, 1859.	Coward, Edward, Assoc. Inst. C.E., M.Inst.M.E.
Nov. 12, 1861.	Coward, Thomas.
April 11, 1781.	Cowling, John, M.D.
Nov. 2, 1810.	Craig, John.
Jan. 26, 1810.	Cririe, William.
April 29, 1851.	Crompton, Samuel, M.D.
Jan. 22, 1859.	Crossley, James, F.S.A.
Nov. 12, 1895.	Crossley, William John, M.Inst.M.E.
Jan. 25, 1848.	Crowther, Joseph Stretch.
Jan. 24, 1854.	Culley, Richard Spelman.
Nov. 1, 1833.	Cumber, Charles.
April 18, 1876.	Cunliffe, Robert Ellis.
April 2, 1861.	Cunningham, William Alexander.
Jan. 22, 1861.	Curtis, John.
April 18, 1843.	Curtis, Matthew.

Oct. 29, 1824.	Dadley, Henry.
Feb. 7, 1854.	Dale, John, F.C.S.
Nov. 28, 1871.	Dale, Richard Samuel, B.A.
April 25, 1794.	Dalton, John, D.C.L., F.R.S.
April 19, 1842.	Dancer, John Benjamin, F.R.A.S.
Feb. 10, 1863.	Darbishire, George Stanley.
April 26, 1811.	Darbishire, James, jun.
April 19, 1853.	Darbishire, Robert Dukinfield, B.A., F.S.A.
Jan. 25, 1822.	Darbishire, Samuel Dukinfield.
Jan. 21, 1862.	Darbishire, William Arthur, B.A.
June 13, 1781.	Darby, Robert, M.D.
Jan. 24, 1854.	Davies, David Reynolds.
Nov. 1, 1816.	Davies, John, M.W.S.
Jan. 21, 1851.	Davies, Rev. John, M.A.
Jan. 24, 1806.	Davis, Jacob.
Nov. 26, 1878.	Davis, Joseph.
Nov. 2, 1869. } April 9, 1895. }	Dawkins, William Boyd, M.A., F.R.S., F.G.S.
April 25, 1794.	Dawson, John Charlton.
Nov. 15, 1870.	Deacon, Henry, F.C.S.
Nov. 15, 1842.	Dean, James Joseph.
Dec. 10, 1861.	Deane, William King.
Jan. 8, 1790.	Delap, Robert.
Mar. 6, 1894.	Delépine, A. Sheridan, M.B., B.Sc.

Date of Election.

Jan. 25, 1853.	Fairbairn, George.
April 30, 1850.	Fairbairn, Sir Thomas, Bart.
Oct. 29, 1824.	Fairbairn, Sir William, Bart., LL.D., F.R.S.
Oct. 30, 1849.	Fairbairn, William Andrew.
Mar. 5, 1878.	Fairgrieve, Andrew.
Oct. 2, 1883.	Faraday, Frederick James, F.L.S., F.S.S.
April 29, 1825.	Fawdington, Thomas.
Jan. 25, 1848.	Ferguson, Pearson Biggs.
April 12, 1786.	Ferriar, John, M.D.
Jan. 26, 1847.	Ferris, Octavius Allen.
Nov. 2, 1810.	Finch, William.
Jan. 27, 1832.	Fincham, Frederick.
Oct. 21, 1851.	Finlay, Robert, B.A.
Jan. 22, 1861.	Fisher, William Henry.
Jan. 25, 1842.	Fleming, David Gibson.
April 30, 1824.	Fleming, Thomas.
April 18, 1828.	Fleming, William, M.D.
Oct. 31, 1817.	Flint, Richard.
April 30, 1895.	Flux, Alfred William, M.A.
April 29, 1856.	Forrest, Henry Robert.
April 24, 1795.	Fosbrooke, Thomas.
April 21, 1857.	Foster, Thomas Barham.
Jan. 23, 1855.	Fothergill, Benjamin.
Mar. 28, 1781.	Foxley, Rev. John.
F. Dec. 1, 1784.	} Foxley, Robinson, M.D.
Nov. 20, 1782.	Foxlow, Thomas Peter.
April 17, 1860.	Francis, John.
April 29, 1851.	Frankland, Edward, Ph.D., D.C.L., F.R.S.
Jan. 22, 1839.	Fraser, James William.
April 16, 1872.	Freeston, Rev. Joseph.
Jan. 24, 1854.	Fryer, Alfred.
Nov. 18, 1873.	Gamgee, Arthur, M.D., F.R.S.
Jan. 25, 1811.	Garforth, James Benjamin.
Jan. 23, 1824.	Garnett, William.
Feb. 6, 1877.	Garnett, William.
Jan. 21, 1840.	Gaskell, Rev. William, M.A.
Oct. 30, 1829.	Gaulter, Henry, M.D.
Feb. 9, 1886.	Gee, William Winson Haldane, B.Sc.
Jan. 25, 1800.	Gibson, Benjamin.
April 29, 1836.	Giles, Samuel.
April 30, 1861.	Gladstone, Murray, F.R.A.S.

Date of Election.

F.	Hall, Edward.
F.	Hall, Richard.
F.	Hall, Richard Edward.
April 18, 1781.	Hall, Rev. Samuel, M.A.
April 29, 1845.	Halley, Rev. Robert, D.D.
Nov. 26, 1790.	Hamilton, Gavin.
Nov. 28, 1865.	Hampson, Francis.
Jan. 23, 1844.	Hampson, Richard.
Oct. 1, 1878.	Hannay, James Ballantyne, F.R.S.E.
Jan. 25, 1800.	Hanson, Edward.
April 25, 1794.	Hanson, Joseph.
April 14, 1896.	Harden, Arthur, M.Sc., Ph.D.
Jan. 24, 1812.	Hardie, Henry, M.D.
Jan. 27, 1837.	Hardy, Robert, M.D.
Nov. 3, 1891.	Hare, Arthur William, M.D., F.R.S.E.
Feb. 18, 1890.	Harker, Thomas.
April 30, 1878.	Harland, William Dugdale, F.C.S.
Oct. 30, 1849.	Harley, Rev. Robert, M.A., F.R.S.
Feb. 9, 1864.	Harris, George, LL.D., F.S.A.
Jan. 7, 1890.	Harrison, Frederick, M.A.
Dec. 5, 1781.	Harrison, Rev. Ralph.
Oct. 3, 1871.	Harrison, Thomas.
April 28, 1797.	Harrison, William.
Oct. 19, 1858.	Harrison, William Philip, M.D.
Nov. 4, 1862.	Hart, Peter.
April 18, 1823.	Hartley, Jesse.
Nov. 12, 1895.	Hartog, Philippe Joseph, B.Sc., F.C.S.
Nov. 26, 1790.	Harvey, Samuel.
Jan. 25, 1793.	Hatfield, Thomas.
April 28, 1809.	Hatfield, Thomas James.
Oct. 21, 1803.	Hawkes, Rev. James.
Nov. 20, 1789.	Hawkes, Rev. William.
Jan. 22, 1839.	Hawkshaw, Sir John, F.R.S., F.G.S.
Jan. 25, 1793.	Hay, Charles.
April 26, 1793.	Hay, William.
April 2, 1861.	Haywood, George Robert.
Dec. 16, 1873.	Heelis, James.
April 19, 1859.	Heelis, Thomas, F.R.A.S.
Nov. 4, 1890.	Heenan, Hammersley, M.Inst.C.E., M.Inst.M E.
Mar. 4, 1890.	Henderson, Herbert Arthur.
Nov. 15, 1842.	Henfrey, Charles.
Jan. 24, 1806.	Hennell, James.
F.	Henry, Thomas, F.R.S.

Ordinary Members.

Date of Election.

Nov. 26, 1878.	Jones, Francis, F.R.S.E., F.C.S.
Dec. 1, 1885.	Jones, Henry, B.A.
April 21, 1846. ⎫ Jan. 22, 1856. ⎭	Jones, Rev. Henry Halford, F.R.A.S.
Nov. 15, 1842.	Jones, Rev. Henry Longueville, M.A., F.R.A.S.
Oct. 19, 1821.	Jordan, Joseph, F.R.C.S.
Jan. 7, 1890.	Joseland, Henry Lincoln, M.A.
April 18, 1848.	Joule, Benjamin St. John Baptist.
Jan. 25, 1842.	Joule, James Prescott, LL,D., D.C.L., F.R.S.
April 1, 1862.	Joy, David.
Nov. 17, 1891.	Joyce, Samuel.
Jan. 27, 1846.	Joynson, William.

Oct. 30, 1818.	Kay, Alexander, jun.
Jan. 23, 1829.	Kay-Shuttleworth, Sir James ⎱ Phillips, Bart., M.D., D.C.L. (M.P.)
Oct. 18, 1799.	Kay, Samuel.
Jan. 24, 1843.	Kay, Samuel, jun.
Jan. 12, 1886.	Kay, Thomas.
Jan. 24, 1817.	Kennedy, James.
April 29, 1803.	Kennedy, John.
Jan. 27, 1852.	Kennedy, John Lawson.
April 18, 1823.	Kennedy, Peter.
June 27, 1781.	Kenyon, Rev. Robert, M.A.
Jan. 24, 1854.	Kershaw, James, jun.
May 16, 1781.	Kershaw, Thomas.
Jan. 25, 1811.	Kinder, Henry.
April 29, 1884.	King, Alfred John, B.Sc., F.C.S.
Dec. 1, 1891.	King, John Edward, M.A.
Nov. 26, 1867.	Kipping, James Stanley.
Oct. 19, 1821.	Kirk, Benjamin.
Nov. 12, 1895.	Kirkman, William Wright.
April 29, 1862.	Knowles, Andrew.
Nov. 19, 1783.	Kuitner, —

Jan. 26, 1827.	Lacy, Henry Charles.
Mar. 9, 1886. ⎫ Nov. 14, 1893. ⎭	Lamb, Horace, M.A., F.R.S.
Oct. 21, 1791.	Lamb, William.
April 27, 1810.	Landor, Thomas.
April 26, 1822.	Lane, Richard.
Nov. 4, 1890.	Langdon, Maurice Julius, Ph.D.

Date of Election.	
April 26, 1799.	Peel, Robert.
Nov. 12, 1802.	Peel, Robert, jun.
Nov. 12, 1895.	Pennington, James Dixon, B.A., B.Sc.
Jan. 13, 1874.	Pennington, Rooke, LL.B., F.G.S.
F.	Percival, Thomas, M.D., F.R.S., F.S.A.
Jan. 23, 1824.	Perigal, Arthur.
Nov. 15, 1892.	Perkin, William Henry, jun., Ph.D., F.R.S., F.C.S.
Jan. 22, 1861.	Perring, John Shae, M.Inst.C.E.
April 13, 1785.	Philips, Sir George, Bart. (M.P.)
Jan. 22, 1783.	Philips, John.
Dec. 26, 1781.	Philips, John Leigh.
Nov. 5, 1783.	Philips, Robert.
Oct. 29, 1830.	Phillips, Charles, M.D.
Nov. 17, 1885.	Phillips, Henry Harcourt, F.C.S.
Nov. 15, 1842.	Phillips, Montague L.
Nov. 10, 1784.	Phillips, Thomas.
Oct. 18, 1799.	Phillips, Waller.
April 28, 1809.	Phipson, W. H.
Nov. 29, 1870.	Piers, Sir Eustace Fitzmaurice, Bart.
Jan. 25, 1848.	Pincoffs, Peter, M.D.
Jan. 22, 1861.	Pincoffs, Simon.
April 21, 1857.	Platt, William Wilkinson.
Jan. 25, 1842.	Playfair, Rt. Hon. Lyon, Lord, K.C.B., F.R.S.
Jan. 24, 1854.	Pochin, Henry Davis, F.C.S. (M.P.)
April 17, 1860.	Pocklington, Rev. Joseph Nelsey, B.A.
F.	Polier (Bottens), Charles de.
April 21, 1826.	Potter, Edmund, F.R.S.
Oct. 22, 1783.	Potter, James.
Jan. 23, 1824.	Potter, John.
Nov. 3, 1784.	Powel, John.
Feb. 6, 1877.	Poynting, John Henry, Sc.D., F.R.S.
Jan. 27, 1857.	Poynting, Rev. Thomas Elford.
Jan. 22, 1819.	Prentice, Archibald.
Jan. 22, 1861.	Preston, Francis.
Jan. 22, 1839.	Price, David.
Oct. 1, 1878.	Priestley, John, M.R.C.S.
Oct. 21, 1791.	Priestley, Joseph, jun.
April 29, 1831.	Pryce, John.
April 26, 1799.	Pye, Charles.
Jan. 25, 1793.	Radcliffe, Rev. John, M.A.
Jan. 22, 1836.	Radford, Joseph.
Jan. 21, 1831.	Radford, Thomas, M.D.

Date of Election.	
	*Rupp, Theophilus Lewis.
Nov. 1, 1793.	Rushforth, Richard.
Jan. 23, 1844.	Rylands, Thomas Glazebrook, F.S.A., F.L.S., F.G.S.
Jan. 21, 1890.	Sacré, Howard C., F.C.S.
April 18, 1848.	Salt, Samuel.
April 29, 1851.	Sandeman, Archibald, M.A.
Nov. 3, 1815.	Sanderson, T. B. W.
Jan. 26, 1816.	Sandford, Benjamin.
Jan, 26, 1847.	Satterthwaite, Michael, M.D.
Oct. 30, 1829.	Saulter, Henry.
Mar. 21, 1893.	Schill, Charles Henry.
April 29, 1831.	Scholes, Thomas Seddon.
Dec. 13, 1870.	Schorlemmer, Carl, LL.D., F.R.S., F.C.S.
Jan. 25, 1842.	Schunck, Edward, Ph.D., F.R.S., F.C.S,
Nov. 18, 1873.	Schuster, Arthur, Ph.D., F.R.S.
April 7, 1863. Nov. 29, 1881.	Schwabe, Edmund Salis, B.A.
April 20, 1847.	Schwabe, Salis.
Feb. 7, 1854.	Scott, Alexander John, M.A.
April 30, 1824.	Sergeant, Edwin W.
Oct. 19, 1858.	Sever, Charles.
Jan. 23, 1855.	Sharp, Edmund Hamilton.
Oct. 29, 1824.	Sharp, John.
April 17, 1838.	Sharp, Rev. John.
Jan. 26, 1816.	Sharp, Thomas.
April 28, 1797.	Sharpe, John.
Jan. 25, 1833.	Shaw, George, M.D.
Nov. 12, 1895.	Shearer, Arthur.
Jan. 24, 1823.	Sherratt, John.
Oct. 30, 1835.	Shuttleworth, John.
April 29, 1851.	Sichel, Ferdinand.
Nov. 4, 1890.	Sidebotham, Edward John, M.A., M.B., M.R.C.S.
Oct. 5, 1886.	Sidebotham, George William, M.R.C.S.
Jan. 21, 1890.	Sidebotham, James Nasmyth, Assoc.M.Inst.C.E.
April 20, 1852.	Sidebotham, Joseph, F.R.A S., F.S.A.
Dec. 4, 1789.	Simmons, William.
April 6, 1886.	Simon, Henry, M.Inst.C.E., M.Inst.M.E.
Dec. 26, 1865.	Simpson, Henry, M.D.
Jan. 25, 1859.	Slagg, John, jun. (M.P.) ·
Nov. 5, 1783.	Slater, Rev. Frederick Robert.

* No record of election, but appears in list of members published in Vol. V., part I. of the "Memoirs" (1798), and is marked as on the Committee of Papers.

Date of Election.	
April 29, 1808.	Taylor, John.
April 18, 1828.	Taylor, John Edward.
Jan. 22, 1856.	Taylor, John Edward, jun.
Nov. 14, 1893.	Taylor, Robert Llewellyn, F.C.S.
Nov. 4, 1890.	Taylor, Walter, A.M.Inst.C.E.
Mar. 22, 1870.	Teale, James.
April 20, 1852.	Thom, David.
Jan. 27, 1846.	Thom, John.
F.	Thomas, —
April 18, 1854.	Thompson, James.
Jan. 25, 1859.	Thompson, James.
April 18, 1823.	Thompson, John Bent.
Mar. 18, 1884.	Thompson, Joseph.
Jan. 23, 1824.	Thompson, William.
Jan. 21, 1820.	Thomson, Edmund Peel.
Jan. 27, 1826.	Thomson, William, M.A.
April 15, 1873.	Thomson, William, F.R.S.E., F.C.S.
Jan. 21, 1896.	Thorburn, William, M.D., B.Sc.
April 30, 1889.	Thornber, Harry.
Jan. 21, 1896.	Thorp, Thomas.
Nov. 3, 1815.	Thorpe, Robert.
Nov. 2, 1869.	Thorpe, Thomas Edward, Ph.D., LL.D., F.R.S., F.C.S.
April 17, 1860.	Trapp, Samuel Clement.
April 29, 1836.	Turner, James Aspinall (M.P.)
April 19, 1821.	Turner, Thomas, F.R.C.S., F.L.S.
Jan. 24, 1860.	Unwin, William Cawthorne, B.Sc., F.R.S., M.Inst.C.E.
April 25, 1794.	Vause, Rev. John, B.A.
Jan. 27, 1832.	Vembergue, Francis Eugene.
April 30, 1861.	Vernon, George Venables, F.R.A.S.
F.	Wakefield, George.
Jan. 30, 1782.	Walker, George.
Dec. 7, 1798.	Walker, Rev. George, F.R.S.
Oct. 19, 1827.	Walker, John Goldie, jun.
Jan. 27, 1857.	Walker, Robert, M.D.
Jan. 22, 1790.	Walker, Thomas.
Jan. 26, 1841.	Wallace, Rev. Robert.
Mar. 5, 1895.	Ward, Adolphus William, Litt.D., LL.D.
Nov. 14, 1882.	Ward, Harry Marshall, M.A., Sc.D., F.R.S.
	*Ward, John.

* No record of election, but appears in list of members published in Vol. III. of the "Memoirs" (1790).

Date of Election.

Oct. 26, 1785.	Ward, Michael, M.D.
Dec. 30, 1879.	Ward, Thomas.
Nov. 18, 1873.	Waters, Arthur William, F.L.S., F.G.S
Jan. 24, 1823.	Watkin, Absalom.
April 26, 1793.	Watkins, James.
Nov. 4, 1873.	Watkins, James.
Jan. 25, 1859.	Watson, John.
Dec. 15, 1874.	Watson, Morrison, M.D., F.R.S,
Jan. 26, 1816.	Watson, Peter.
Feb. 6, 1789.	Watt, James, jun.
Jan. 27, 1874.	Watts, John, Ph.D.
Dec. 29, 1868.	Watts, William Marshall, D.Sc.
Jan. 27, 1857.	Webb, Thomas George.
Nov. 15, 1892.	Weiss, Frederick Ernest, B.Sc., F.L.S.
April 30, 1802.	Welshman, John Walter.
Oct. 15, 1861.	Whalley, John.
Jan. 25, 1822.	Whatton, William Robert, F.R.S., F.S.A.
Jan. 25, 1828.	Wheeler, Thomas.
April 26, 1811.	White, Arthur Bourne.
F.	White, Charles, F.R.S.
Mar. 28, 1781.	White, John.
April 20, 1792.	White, John Bradshaw.
Oct. 26, 1785.	White, Thomas, M.D.
F.	White, William.
Jan. 26, 1858.	Whitehead, James, M.D., F.R.C.S.
April 9, 1895.	Whitehead, James.
Feb. 9, 1869.	Whitehead, Walter, M.R.C.S.
Jan. 23, 1782.	Whittaker, James.
Jan. 22, 1839.	Whitworth, Sir Joseph, Bart., D.C.L., F.R.S.
Oct. 19, 1847.	Wightman, Alexander.
Jan. 25, 1842.	Wild, Charles Heard.
Jan. 25, 1859.	Wilde, Henry, F.R.S.
Dec. 29, 1868.	Wilkins, Augustus Samuel, M.A., Litt.D.
Jan. 26, 1841.	Wilkinson, Matthew Alexander Eason, M.D.
Jan. 26, 1821.	Wilkinson, Thomas Jones.
April 19, 1859.	Wilkinson, Thomas Read.
Nov. 12, 1889.	Willans, John William.
April 17, 1888.	Williams, Sir Edward Leader, M.Inst.C.E., M.Inst,M.E.
Nov. 3, 1874.	Williams, William Carleton, B.Sc., F.C.S.
April 19, 1887.	Williamson, J. H. R.
April 19, 1853.	Williamson, Samuel Walker.
April 29, 1851.	Williamson, William Crawford, LL.D., F.R.S.
April 25, 1781.	Wilson, John.

Date of Election.	
April 16, 1889.	Wilson, Thomas Bright, A.M.Inst.C.E.
April 29, 1814.	Wilson, William James, F.R.C.S.
Nov. 28, 1781.	Wimpey, Joseph.
Mar. 8, 1864.	Windsor, Thomas, M.R.C.S.
Oct. 31, 1871.	Winstanley, David, F.R.A.S.
Jan. 26, 1841.	Winstanley, Thomas Woodcock.
Jan. 23, 1807.	Winstanley, William, M.D.
Nov. 2, 1810.	Winter, Gilbert.
Jan. 27, 1851.	Withington, George.
Jan. 21, 1851.	Withington, George Bancroft.
Oct. 16, 1801.	Wood, Charles.
April 24, 1807.	Wood, George William, F.L.S., F.G.S. (M.P.)
Jan. 22, 1819.	Wood, Kinder.
Jan. 22, 1783.	Wood, Ottiwell, jun.
Jan. 22, 1836.	Wood, William Rayner.
Oct. 30, 1855.	Woodcock, Alonzo Buonaparte.
⸀an. 26, 1841.	Woodcroft, Bennett, F.R.S.
April 17, 1860.	Woodcroft, Rufus Dewar.
April 21, 1846.	Woodhead, George.
April 30, 1839.	Woods, Edward.
April 17, 1860.	Woolley, George Stephen.
Nov. 15, 1842.	Woolley, James.
Jan. 21, 1896.	Wordingham, Charles Henry, A.M.Inst.C.E.
Oct. 29, 1819.	Worthington, Henry Robert.
April 28, 1840.	Worthington, Robert, F.R.A.S.
Nov. 17, 1863.	Worthington, Samuel Barton, M.Inst.C.E., M.Inst.M.E.
Feb. 21, 1865.	Worthington, Thomas, F.R.I.B.A.
Jan. 8, 1895.	Worthington, William Barton, B.Sc., M.Inst.C.E.
F.	Wright, John, M.D.
Nov. 1, 1864.	Wright, William Cort, F.C.S.
Nov. 9, 1785.	Wynne, John.
Nov. 13, 1795.	Yates, Joseph.
Jan. 26, 1841.	Yates, Joseph St. John.
April 26, 1799.	Yates, Thomas.
Oct. 19, 1847.	Young, James, LL.D., F.R.S.

LIST OF MS. RECORDS AND PUBLICATIONS.

MANUSCRIPT VOLUMES.

JOURNALS.

1. From February 28, 1781, to February 13, 1782,
2. „ February 6, 1782, to March 17, 1784.
3. „ March 24, 1784, to April 29, 1791.
4. „ October 7, 1791, to December 27, 1799.
5. „ January 10, 1800, to March 4, 1808.
6. „ March 18, 1808, to January 9, 1818.
7. „ January 23, 1818, to January 25, 1828.
8. „ February 8, 1828, to March 5, 1836.
9. „ March 18, 1836, to December 28, 1841.
10. „ January 11, 1842, to May 5, 1846.
11. „ October 6, 1846, to May 2, 1854.
12. „ October 3, 1854, to April 19, 1864.

MINUTES OF THE COUNCIL.

1. From March 18, 1851, to January 8, 1867.
2. „ February 5, 1867, to March 8, 1892.
3. „ April 5, 1892, to present time.

PROPOSAL BOOKS.

1. From January 24, 1794, to November 1, 1816.
2. „ January 24, 1817, to April 28, 1840.
3. „ April 28, 1840, to January 25, 1859.
4. „ January 25, 1859, to January 12, 1886.
5. „ February 9, 1886, to present time.

PUBLICATIONS.

MEMOIRS, FIRST SERIES. 8vo.

Vol. I.* (1785) 24+473+11 pp., 3 pl.
„ I. (2nd ed.) (1789) 24+473+10 pp., 3 pl.
„ II.* (1785) 9+514+12 pp., 2 pl.
„ II. (2nd ed.) (1789) 8+530+13 pp., 2 pl.
„ III. (1790) 16+648[+24-31]+12 pp., 5 pl.
„ IV. pt. 1. (1793) 16+272 pp., 3 pl., 3 tables.
„ IV. „ 2. (1796) 7+273-653+3 pp., 6 pl.
„ V. „ 1. (1798) 16+318 pp., 4 pl.
„ V. „ 2. (1802) 7+319-700 pp., 5 pl.

* Vols. I. and II. were also translated and printed in German under the title:
"Physikalische und philosophische Abhandlungen der Gesellschaft der Wissenschaften
zu Manchester." Theil I. und II. 8vo., *Leipzig*, 1783.

MEMOIRS, SECOND SERIES. 8vo.

Vol. I. (1805) 15+442 pp., 3 pl.
„ II. (1813) 8+484 pp., 9 pl.
„ III. (1819) 8+512 pp., 2 pl.
„ IV. (1824) 4+528 pp., 4 pl., 1 table.
„ V. (1831) 8+2+564 pp., 2 pl.
„ VI. (1842) 9+632+9+8 pp., 16 pl., 1 map, 2 tables.
  „ VII. (1846) 11+676+8+19 pp., 4 pl.
„ VIII. (1848) 9+8+8+476+5 pp., 9 pl.
„ IX. (1851) 8+376 pp., 6 pl.
„ X. (1852) 7+231 pp., 2 pl.
„ XI. (1854) 7+224 pp., 1 pl.
„ XII. (1855) 7+324+2 pp.
„ XIII. (1856) Memoir of John Dalton. By R. Angus Smith.
       3+7+298 pp., 1 port.
„ XIV. (1857) 7+266 pp., 2 pl.
„ XV. (1860) 8+316+34+30 pp., 2 pl., 1 table.

MEMOIRS, THIRD SERIES. 8vo.

Vol. I. (1862) 8+423+42+20 pp., 15 pl.
„ II. (1865) 8+464+16 pp., 13 pl.
„ III. (1868) 7+313+15 pp., 7 pl.
„ IV. (1871) 7+352+15 pp., 8 pl.
„ V. (1876) 8+369+14 pp., 3 pl.
„ VI. (1879) 8+278+12 pp., 1 port.
„ VII. (1882) 8+201+10 pp., 1 table.
„ VIII. (1884) 8+229+10 pp., 20 pl.
„ IX. (1883) A Centenary of Science in Manchester. By R. Angus
       Smith. 12+475 pp.
  X. (1887) 7+271+11 pp., 16 pl., 2 tables.

MEMOIRS AND PROCEEDINGS, FOURTH SERIES. 8vo.

Vol. I. (1888) 8+282 pp., 2 pl.
„ II. (1889) 8+281 pp., 1 pl.
„ III. (1890) 7+332 pp., 10 pl.
„ IV. (1891) 10+505 pp., 4 pl.
„ V. (1892) 7+208 pp., 4 pl.
„ VI. (1892) Memoir of J. P. Joule. By O. Reynolds.
       8+196 pp., 1 port.
„ VII. (1893) 7+262 pp., 1 pl.
„ VIII. (1894) 8+236 pp., 10 pl., 1 map.
„ IX. (1895) 7+259 pp., 6 pl., 1 table.
„ X. (1896) 6+158 pp., 3 pl.

NOTE.—*Forty volumes of Memoirs have been issued since the commencement; the volumes will for the future be numbered XLI., XLII., &c., and not according to Series.*

PROCEEDINGS. 8vo.

Vol. I., 1857-60 [1860] 8+261 pp., 3 pl.
„   II., 1860-62 (1862) 2+268 pp.
„   III., 1862-64 (1864) 9+280 pp.
„   IV., 1864-65 (1865) 8+208 pp.
„   V., 1865-66 (1866) 8+194 pp., 1 pl.
„   VI., 1866-67 (1867) 8+196 pp.
„   VII., 1867-68 (1868) 7+224 pp.
„   VIII., 1868-69 (1869) 8+206 pp.
„   IX., 1869-70 (1870) 7+195 pp.
„   X., 1870-71 (1871) 7+219 pp.
„   XI., 1871-72 (1872) 7+188 pp.
„   XII., 1872-73 (1873) 7+150 pp.
„   XIII., 1873-74 (1874) 7+178 pp.
„   XIV., 1874-75 (1875) 7+155 pp.
„   XV., 1875-76 (1876) 8+184 pp.
„   XVI., 1876-77 (1877) 8+248 pp.
„   XVII., 1877-78 (1878) 7+230 pp., 1 table
„   XVIII., 1878-79 (1879) 7+150 pp., 1 pl.
„   XIX., 1879-80 (1880) 7+212 pp.
„   XX., 1880-81 (1881) 7+150 pp.
„   XXI., 1881-82 (1882) 7+192 pp.
„   XXII., 1882-83 (1883) 7+105 pp.
„   XXIII., 1883-84 (1884) 7+129+2 pp.
„   XXIV., 1884-85 (1885) 7+113+3 pp.
„   XXV., 1885-86 (1886) 7+250 pp., 4 pl., 1 table.
„   XXVI., 1886-87 (1887) 7+182 pp., 4 pl.

MISCELLANEOUS PUBLICATIONS.

Rules established for the government of the...Society...and a list of the members. 4to., 1782.

A short account of the institution and views of the...Society, *etc.* 4to., [1783?]

——[Another edition.] 4to., [1784?]

Rules. 8 pp. 8vo., 1852.

——[Another edition.] 14 pp. 8vo., 1861.

Memorandum of Association and Articles of Association. 20+1 p fol., 1875.

——[Another edition.] 20+1 pp. fol., 1891.

——[Another edition, revised.] 31 pp. 8vo., 1895.

Catalogue of the books in the library. 18+1 pp. 8vo., 1840.

Catalogue of the library. 24+1 pp. 8vo., 1845.

Alphabetical catalogue of the books and journals in the library.. Prepared by T. Windsor. 3+72 pp. 8vo., 1865.

Catalogue of the books in the library...[By] F. Nicholson, Hon. Librarian. 3+173 pp.. 8vo., 1875.

43

APPENDIX I.

———⌐———

(Title Page.) RULES, established for the government of the LITERARY and PHILOSOPHICAL SOCIETY of Manchester; and a List of the Members. Manchester: Printed by Charles Wheeler, 1782.

RULES, established for the government of the LITERARY and PHILOSOPHICAL SOCIETY of Manchester. ⅃

1. THAT this Society be called the LITERARY and PHILO-SOPHICAL SOCIETY of MANCHESTER.

2. That the number of Members be limited to fifty: but this limitation shall not preclude any number of gentlemen, distinguished for their literary or philosophical abilities, and residing at such distances from *Manchester* as to prevent their attendance at the usual meetings of the Society, from being elected *honorary* Members; provided the mode of recommendation and election be the same, in other respects, as that of the ordinary Members, hereafter to be described.

3. That every Candidate for admission into the Society shall be proposed by at least three Members, who shall sign a Certificate of his being, from their knowledge of him or his writings, a fit person to be admitted into the Society; which certificate shall be hung up during four successive meetings of the Society, in the room where the meetings are held; and the name of the Candidate shall be read up by the Secretary, at each meeting of the Society, during that period.

4. That every election of a new Member into the Society shall be decided by ballot. That no less a number than thirteen Members shall proceed to election, and that a majority of votes of the Members present in favour of the Candidate, shall be requisite for his admission. The President to have a casting voice, if the number of votes be equal.

5. That two Presidents, four Vice-Presidents, and two Secretaries shall be elected annually, by the majority of the members present, on the last *Wednesday* which shall happen in the month of *April*. The election to be determined by ballot.

6. That a Committee of Papers be appointed at the same time, which shall consist of the Presidents, Vice-Presidents, Secretaries, and six other Members of the Society, to be chosen by ballot. And that this Committee shall decide, by ballot, concerning the insertion, in the Register, of any paper which shall have been read before the Society; and shall be authorised to select, with the consent of the author, detached parts of any paper, the whole of which may not be deemed proper for insertion. But that it shall be requisite, that at least seven Members of the Committee attend at the discussion and decision upon each paper.

7. That any Member may introduce a stranger, *viz.*, a gentleman not residing in *Manchester*, at the meetings of the Society, having first obtained leave of the President, by sending up the name of the stranger.

8. That each Member of the Society shall be allowed to introduce a visitor, being an inhabitant of Manchester, provided he give notice of it to the acting Secretary on or before the day previous to the Meeting. But this privilege shall not be enjoyed by more than three Members at one time, and no Member shall avail himself of it twice within the space of eight Meetings.

9. That the subjects of conversation comprehended Natural Philosophy, Theoretical and Experimental Chemistry, Polite Literature, Civil Law, General Politics, Commerce, and the Arts. But that Religion, the Practical Branches of Physic, and *British* Politics, be deemed prohibited subjects of conversation; and that the Chairman shall deliver his *veto* whenever they are introduced.

10. That each Member who shall favour the Society with any interesting facts and observations, respecting philosophy, polite literature, *&c.*, which may occur to him, either from reflection, experiment, reading or correspondence, shall send or deliver his paper to one of the Secretaries, the *Monday* before the Meeting of the Society.

11. That the Secretary to whom the paper shall be delivered, shall, with the approbation of one President or two Vice-

Presidents, have the power of suspending the recital of it, if deemed improper to be read, till the pleasure of the Committee of Papers concerning it be known, a meeting of which shall be called by the Secretary to inspect it; and in case the Committee disapprove of its being introduced to the Society, they be impowered to issue their *veto* against it.

12. That all papers which shall be delivered in to the Secretary, and not prohibited as above, shall be read by him or the author, according to the order of succession in which they were presented.

13. That each paper shall be read to the Society without interruption, and that more than 15 minutes shall not be allowed to the reading of any single paper; but if the length of it require more time in the delivery, the remainder shall, except the Society determine otherwise, be deferred to the succeeding meeting.

14. That a second paper shall not be read before the subject of the former one has been discussed.

15. That no tea, coffee, or other liquors be permitted to be introduced at the weekly meetings of the Society.

16. That the days on which the Society shall meet, be every *Wednesday* in the Year, excepting during the months of *June, July,* and *August,* during which time, the meetings shall be confined to the first *Wednesday* in each of the said months; and that each meeting shall commence at six o'clock, and be concluded at eight o'clock in the evening.

17. That each Member shall pay One Guinea annually, at half yearly payments, into the hands of one of the Secretaries, to be applied to defray the rent of the room, and other incidental expences; and if any Member shall refuse or neglect to pay his Subscription, he shall be excluded the Society. Each Member, on his election, to pay his Subscription for the current half year.

18. That it be recommended to each Member to enter the Society's room with silence, and without ceremony.

19. That no laws be enacted, rescinded or altered but at the meetings on the last *Wednesdays* which shall happen in the months of *January, April,* and *October;* nor without notice being given, at least fourteen days, previous to those meetings.

A LIST OF THE MEMBERS

OF THE

LITERARY AND PHILOSOPHICAL SOCIETY OF MANCHESTER.

*James Massey, Esq.
*Thomas Percival, M.D., F.R.S., & S.A., } PRESIDENTS.
and Reg. Soc. Med. Par. Soc.

*The Rev. Thomas Barnes.
*Alexander Eason, M.D. } VICE-
*John Cowling, M.D. } PRESIDENTS.
*The Rev. Samuel Hall, A.M.

*Mr. Thomas Henry, F.R.S. } SECRETARIES.
*Mr. George Bew.

Mr. James Ashworth.	George Lloyd, Esq.
Mr. John Barrow.	Peter Mainwaring, M.D.
Thomas B. Bayley, Esq., F.R.S.	Mr. John Massey.
*George Bell, M.D.	Mr. Isaac Moss.
*The Rev. John Bennet.	Mr. John Nanfan.
Mr. John Birch.	Mr. Joshua Oldham.
Mr. Ashworth Clegg.	Mr. John Orme.
Mr. Robert Darbey.	Mr. John Leigh Philips.
Mr. James Dinwiddie.	*Charles de Polier, Esq.
Mr. John Drinkwater.	The Rev. William Rankin.
Mr. George Duckworth.	Mr. William Reid.
The Rev. John Foxley, A.M.	William Roberton, Esq.
Mr. Robinson Foxley.	Mr. Thomas Robinson.
The Rev. Peter Haddon, A.M.	*Mr. Charles Taylor.
Mr. Richard Edward Hall.	Mr. George Wakefield.
Mr. Edward Hall.	Mr. George Walker.
Mr. Richard Hall.	Mr. James Whitaker.
The Rev. Ralph Harrison.	*Charles White, Esq., F.R.S.
The Rev. William Hoghton.	Mr. John Wilson.
The Rev. Robert Kenyon, A.M.	*Mr. John Wimpey.
Mr. Thomas Kershaw.	John Wright, M.D.

HONORARY MEMBERS.

Mr. John Aikin.	Mr. Patrick M'Morland.
James Currie, M.D.	Henry Moyes, M.D.
The Rev. William Enfield, LL.D.	The Rev. Joseph Priestley, LL.D.,
John Haygarth, M.D., F.R.S.	F.R.S., Ac. R. Holm. Soc.
William Hawes, M.D.	Dorning Rasbotham, Esq.
Mr. George Hibbert.	Samuel Foart Simmons, M.D., F.R.S.,
John Coakley Lettsom, M.D., F.R.S.,	R.S. Med. Par. Soc., and Soc. R.
and S.A.	Monspel. Corresp.
Mr. J. H. de Magellan, F.R.S., Acad.	The Rev. George Travis, A.M.
Imp. Petrop., and Reg. Madrit.	The Rev. John Whitaker, B.D., F A.S.
Soc.	

Those Members whose names are marked thus * are of the Committee of Papers.

APPENDIX II.

(Title-page.) A Short Account of the Institution and Views of the LITERARY and PHILOSOPHICAL SOCIETY of MAN-CHESTER. [1783?]

The numerous societies for the promotion of Literature and Philosophy, which have been formed in different parts of Europe, in the course of the last and present centuries, have been not only the means of diffusing knowledge more extensively, but have contributed to produce a greater number of important discoveries, than have been effected in any other equal space of time.

The progress that has been made in Physics and the Belles Lettres, owes its rapidity, if not its origin, to the encouragement which these societies have given to such pursuits, and to the emulation which has been excited between different academical bodies, as well as among the individual members of each institution. The collecting and publishing the more important communications which have been delivered to them, have saved from oblivion many very valuable discoveries, or improvements in arts, and much useful information in the various branches of science. These their modest authors might have been tempted to suppress, but for the respectable sanction of societies of men of the first eminence and learning in their respective countries, and the easy mode of publishing which their volumes of Transactions afford.

Though in France, societies for these purposes have been instituted in several of the Provinces; in England, they have been almost confined to the Capital; and however great have been the advantages resulting from the researches of the learned bodies who are incorporated in London, it seems probable, that the great end of their institutions, the promotion of arts and sciences, may be more widely extended by the forming of Societies, with similar views, in the principal towns in this kingdom.

Men, however great their learning, often become indolent, and unambitious to improve in knowledge, for want of associating with others of similar talents and acquirements. Having few oppor-

tunities of communicating their ideas, they are not very solicitous
to collect or arrange those they have acquired, and are still less
anxious about the further cultivation of their minds. But science,
like fire, is put in motion by collision. Where a number of such
men have frequent opportunities of meeting and conversing
together, thought begets thought, and every hint is turned to
advantage. A spirit of inquiry glows in every breast, each new
discovery relative to the natural, intellectual or moral world
leads to a farther investigation, and each man ardently pants to
distinguish himself in the interesting pursuit.

Such have been the considerations that have led to the institution of the Literary and Philosophical Society of Manchester.
Many years since a few gentlemen, inhabitants of the town, who
were inspired with a taste for Literature and Philosophy, formed
themselves into a kind of weekly club, for the purpose of conversing
on subjects of that nature. These meetings were continued, with
some interruption, for several years, and many respectable persons
being desirous of becoming members, our numbers were soon
increased so far, as to induce the founders of the society to think
of extending their original design. Presidents, and other officers
were elected, a code of laws formed, and a regular society consti-
tuted, and denominated The LITERARY and PHILOSOPHICAL SOCIETY
of MANCHESTER.

It was hoped, that among a number of learned and ingenious
men, not only much useful and entertaining conversation might
arise, but that many interesting communications would be supplied.
Nor has the event disappointed our expectations. Many essays on
important subjects, such as, perhaps, would not disgrace the elder
Societies of Europe, have been written by our members, and read
at our meetings. Several gentlemen of distinguished literary repu-
tation, in distant parts of the kingdom, have favoured us with their
correspondence, and many such characters grace the list of our
honorary members.

That some idea may be formed of the progress our Society has
made, and of the nature of our views, the following list of papers
which have been read before the Society since its institution in
February, 1781, is subjoined; and, it is hoped, may induce men of
knowledge to favour us with communications on any of the following
subjects, viz. Natural Philosophy, Theoretical and Experimental
Chemistry, Polite Literature, Civil Law, *General* Politics, Commerce

and the Arts. Essays on these topics, after they have been read, are submitted, not to petulant criticism, but to the amicable and well-regulated discussion of the Society.

Titles of Papers which have been read at the Meetings of the Literary and Philosophical Society of Manchester :—

1st. Observations on Mr. Norris's account of the Harmattan; by Alexander Eason, M.D.

2d. Observations on the application of Natural History to Poetry; by Thomas Percival, M.D., F.R.S., and S.A., member of the Royal Society of Medicine, at Paris, &c.

3d. Remarks on the power of the human body to resist heat; by George Bell, M.D.

4th. An account of some curious effects produced by air, heated to a great degree, on Thermometers exposed to it; by Thomas Henry, F.R.S., together with copies of letters to Mr. Henry, from Mr. Charles Taylor, and Mr. Thomas Smith.

5th. A moral essay on the advantages which may result from the institution and well regulated support of the Literary and Philosophical Society; by John Wright, M.D. .

6th. An essay on the pleasures arising from minute observation, and the advantages thence arising to the arts; by Mr. Charles Taylor.

7th. A letter from James Massey, Esq., to Mr. Bew, containing a new and simple method of impregnating water with fixed air, with a drawing of the apparatus for that purpose, as well as decomposing lime water.

8th. Some account of the tea tree; by the Rev. John Foxley, A.M.

9th. An essay on the properest methods of publicly rewarding useful discoveries and inventions; by the Rev. Thomas Barnes.

10th. On the advantages of literature and philosophy in general, and especially on the consistency of literary and philosophical, with commercial pursuits; by Thomas Henry, F.R.S.

11th. On the use of patents; by Alexander Eason, M.D.

12th. On association and habit; by Thomas Percival, M.D., F.R.S., &c.

13th. On the pleasures arising from a survey of nature, and conclusions consequent therefrom by Mr. John Wilson.

14th. On crystallization; by Alexander Eason, M.D.

15th. On the preservation of sea water from putrefaction, by means of quick lime, with chemical observations; by Thomas Henry, F.R.S. And also an account of a newly invented machine for impregnating water or other fluids with fixed air; communicated to Mr. Henry, by John Haygarth, M.B., F.R.S.

16th. On the nature and essential character of poetry, as distinguished from prose; by the Rev. Thomas Barnes.

17th. Experiments on the respiration of animals, and the changes effected in the air, in passing thro' the lungs, by Mr. Lavoisier, translated from the Memoirs of the Royal Academy of Sciences for the year 1777, by Thomas Henry, F.R.S.

18th. An essay on the combustion of phosphorus, and the formation of its acid, by the same; translated by Mr. Henry.

19th. On the comparative improvement of the intellectual and moral powers of man in the present and future stages of his being by Thomas Percival, M.D., F.R.S., &c.

20th. Extract of a letter from the Rev. Dr. Griffiths, of St. Mary Hill, to Dr. Percival, containing an account of the Chinese Whang at Tong, lately in London, and an explanation of the Chinese characters, which are marked on a stick of Indian ink.

21st. On the affinity subsisting between the arts, with a plan for promoting and extending our manufactures, by encouraging those arts on which they principally depend; by the Rev. Thomas Barnes.

22d. Remarks on the different success, with respect to health, of some attempts to pass the winter in high northern latitudes; by Mr. John Aikin.

23d. An essay on the formation of saltpetre; by James Massey, Esq.

24th. A letter to James Massey, Esq., on the formation of saltpetre: by Mr. Charles Taylor.

25th. On the existence of air in the nitrous acid, and the means of decomposing and recomposing that acid; by M. Lavoisier, translated by Thomas Henry, F.R.S.

26th. Translation of an eulogy on the late Dr. Haller; by Mr. Henry.

27th. Some remarks on fermentation and putrefaction, and on the influence of the air on them; by Mr. Wimpey.

28th. Speculations on the above paper; by Thomas Percival, M.D., &c.

29th. On the pleasures which the mind receives from the exercise of its faculties, and that of taste in particular; by Charles de Polier, Esq.

30th. Observations on the expediency of œconomical registers; by Mr. Wimpey.

31st. On light and colours; by Mr. Wilson.

32d. On the moral advantages of a taste for the beauties of nature; by Thomas Percival, M.D., &c.

33d. An attempt to account for the pleasure which the mind feels from the contemplation of scenes of distress; by the Rev. Thomas Barnes.

34th. Considerations on taste; by Mr. Wimpey.

35th. A physiological essay on melancholy; by James Currie, M.D.

36th. Observations on blindness, and on the application of the other senses to supply the loss of sight; by Mr. George Bew.

37th. An essay to ascertain the merit of the question respecting vision, formerly discussed by Mr. Locke and Mr. Molyneux, with some remarks on light and colours; by Mr. Wimpey.

38th. An attempt to show that a fine taste for the beauties of nature or of art, has no influence favourable to morals; by the Rev. Samuel Hall, A.M.

39th. On the origin of Government; by Mr. John Buchanan.

40th. A letter from Mr. Wimpey to Mr. Edmund Rack, respecting the use of fallowing.

41st. A supplement to ditto, by ditto.

42d. Observations on the use of acids, in bleaching of linen; by Alexander Eason, M.D.

43d. Conjectural remarks on the symbols or characters employed by the astronomers, to represent the several planets, and by the chemists to express the several metals in a letter to Dr. Percival; by Martin Wall, M.D. and Prælector of Chemistry in the University of Oxford.

44th. Remarks on the knowledge of the ancients by William Falconer, M.D., F.R.S.

45th. On the Influence which the scenery of a country may have on the manners of its inhabitants; by the same.

46th. On the alliance of natural history and philosophy with poetry; by Thomas Percival, M.D., &c.

47th. A tribute to the memory of Charles de Polier, Esq.; by the same.

48th. An essay on the ascent of vapour; by Alexander Eason, M.D.

49th. On the natural and chemical history of magnesian earth; by Thos. Henry. F.R.S. And also a letter from Mr. J. H. de Magellan, F.R.S., &c., to Mr. Henry, on the infusibility of that earth.

50th. Thoughts on evaporation and electricity; by John Mitchell, M.D.

51st. Thoughts on the stile and taste of gardening among the ancients; by William Falconer, M.D., &c.

52d. On the regeneration of animal substances; by Charles White, Esq., F.R.S.

53d. A letter from Dr. Houlston, to Mr. Henry, relating a case in natural history.

54th. An essay on the diversions of hunting, shooting, and fishing, considered as compatible with humanity: by Mr. J. Rathbone.

55th. Observations on longevity; by A. Fothergill, M.D., F.R.S.

The following additional RULES were agreed to, at the Quarterly Meeting of the Society, *January* 29th, 1783:—

That the society shall publish a volume of miscellaneous papers every two years; and that the committee of papers, shall, at the annual meeting in *April*, 1784, select from among the papers which shall have been read to the society, such as shall appear to them most worthy of publication; but if the respective authors shall have expressed a desire that their particular paper or papers may not be published, that, in such case, the printing of such particular paper be not persisted in.

That a Treasurer be added to the officers to be elected at the next annual meeting; and that the accounts be produced, to lye upon the table, at each quarterly meeting.

That no honorary member be proposed, who has not either distinguished himself by his literary or philosophical publications, or favoured the society with some communication, which shall have received the approbation of the committee of papers.

That any person who may be elected a member of this society, after the next annual meeting in *April,* 1783, shall be subject to the depositing of one pound one shilling, as an admission fee, exclusive of the current half yearly subscription.

N.B. In the last printed copy of the rules of the society, the tenth rule should stand in the following form :—

That each member who shall favour the society with any interesting facts and observations, respecting philosophy, polite literature, &c., which may occur to him, either from reflection, experiment, reading or correspondence, shall send or deliver his paper to one of the secretaries, at least ten days revious to its being read before the society.

FINIS

" MANCHESTER GUARDIAN PRINTING WORKS, BLACKFRIARS STREET.